Lessons on Sleeping Alone

Lessons on Sleeping Alone

poems by
Megan E. Freeman

Liquid Light Press
Premium Chapbook First Edition
Copyright © 2015

ISBN-10: 0990926761

ISBN-13: 978-0-9909267-6-4

Liquid Light Press

poetry for the heart

www.liquidlightpress.com

Book design: M. D. Friedman

Cover painting: *Tea for One*, Chuck Ceraso, courtesy of the artist

Author photo: Virginia Jochems Downey

for Georgia and Ameen Alwan,
who cracked open the world
of poetry and invited me in
and
for Jennifer and Alice,
who offered their hands
on the journey inward
and homeward

Contents

Not Unlike Daphne

forsythia grows
from my broken bones

unkempt boughs
of raucous sunshine

noisy herald
of inevitable spring

nothing more
nothing left

but bony branches
budding

as Persephone
steps toward the light

I bloom
into a thousand yellows

exploding new beginnings

have you ever been alone in a city?
secretly writing the names of everyone
who loves you under the jacket
of the Big Book of Alcoholics Anonymous?
propped up and weeping against a motel pillow
hiding from the motel maid?

has the phone ever rung just as you
were writing the name of the boy
in the Spanish class you took as a senior
because your major was complete and
your boyfriend was in Mexico?

have you ever let it ring and ring and ring
and ring until at last it stopped and the little
red light started blinking and clicking?

have you ever ridden in a getaway car
next to a boy — an older boy
who didn't know about Mexican infidelities —
speeding toward the coast
trailing ribbons of colored light and bouncing
a dog-eared copy of *The Stranger*
off the dashboard?

has your heart ever stopped?
exploding in the face of a freedom
never mentioned by guidance counselors
or college professors? unfolding like
a map of Route 66 and a full tank of gas
the promise of kitsch and kinship
just around the bend? Welcome. You Are Here.

Conception, 1967

She woke to webs of valentines strung across the ceiling
above their married-two-years/wedding-night-virgins double bed.

    I waited patiently, weighing different combinations
    of fatherly eloquence and motherly love,
    trying on traits like discount shoes,
    leaving them in piles in the aisles of infinity.

He hung them while she slept, romantic spider with big, thick hands,
spinning silk of paper and scotch tape.

    I waited patiently, studying tintypes and photographs,
    maps of Germany and the British Isles,
    reading names and passports,
    ignoring the stillness and impossibility of time.

The red hearts circulated gently in the easy February air
whispering promises that would, as it turned out, last a lifetime.

    I waited patiently, until, I began,
    exploding in a symphony of cytoplasm,
    splitting and multiplying in deafening combinations of electrical
        impulses.
    Crafting instantly my list of things to do and people to love,
    already onto the second page before my mother's breathing
        slowed
    and her laughter bounced off woven paper hearts
    to germinate the nucleus of me.

Creation Myth

the sharp tip of my arrowhead sternum
the crevices of my shadowy clavicles
the steep edges of my pelvic cradle
(which when held simultaneously
serve to demonstrate the limits of myself)
are points like stars
which when connected by straight lines
create the constellation Metaphor
long worshipped by ancient sages
and the subject of much mythology

Flower Memory

I grew up in the shadow of a paint-splattered rock,
the City of Roses' ugly stepsister-town.
The streets were lined with tassels and diplomas,
and tissue paper flowers spray-painted pink and green.

Sycamore trees grew velvet bark and balls of soft seeds,
easily broken open with nail-bitten thumbs.

Jacaranda blossoms tangled in our skates
and we balanced on the precipice between visibility
and death, trying to impress our younger comrades.

We carefully picked magnolia blossoms
avoiding their tender petals with our dangerous hands,
stroking the seed pods like pincushions sticky with honey
or pomegranates offered and eaten by foolish goddesses.

In bed in the dark with the counterweighted windows
propped open by dictionaries and copies of *Little Women*,
the echo of the marching band ricocheted off institutional walls
providing a cadence by which to fall asleep. The scent
of gardenias placed in bowls on the windowsills
wafted over our dreaming faces and after the drums died away
the coyotes' cries began. Neighbors sought their dogs and cats,
often with success, though occasionally found half-dead
in the driveways with puncture wounds around their ribs.

We were never afraid of Virginia Woolf
and we inherited the wind of the spoken form
which we then transformed into gales of hope
that blew our spores in all directions
to root in the shadows of rocks far away.

The Argument for Ismene

godchild of tragedy

abandoned by violence
orphaned by fate and folly

insignificant life in the noisy epidemic of death
unexamined and forgotten

(the limit was three onstage)

despised in your loyalty
betrayed in your duty

flee to the hills and hide
where your mother's son was left to die

make camp
in your sister's tomb
use the stone on which she stood
to rest your head

suicide is so obvious
but hanging's been done
        twice

mutilation perhaps?
popular also
but spare your five senses please

(disabilities are not practical on the streets of Thebes)

make a marriage with insanity
and languish there
pillaged, raped and plundered of your wits

or rise
rise clear and stoic
free from the burden of doubt

bathe and cleanse yourself of the curse
      (you could teach Eve a thing or two)

stand in the crown
and rule with the wisdom of the wretched
      the war-torn
      the battle-scarred

keen for the lost
and wail for the frailty of foolish kings

but rise
rise and seize
the city with both fists

take the muslin from
around your sister's throat
and twist it through your hair

fasten your mother's brooch
      (still caked with your father's blood)
above your heart
and bear the weight

make a bracelet
from your brothers'
knuckle bones
and feel it slide between your wrist
and the arm of the throne

let your undiluted blood
surge through your
noble veins
giving pride to fire

Breathe in the polluted
breath of sorrow
and exhale the blessing of the pantheon.

It's time to clean house.

it's 1983 again

and I'm fifteen and a half

learning to live above the arctic circle

in half years of darkness and light

reflectors on our clothes

for hiking up to school

aurora borealis skating overhead

as we skated down below

on frozen fields

the most desolate of years

with no one but Johns Irving and Updike

for company

and the post carrying three weeks of wishes

across 10,000 miles of homesick

intimate relationships with chocolate

and one night stands with cigarettes

playing at being human

masquerading in the snow

I stuck pins in the bubbled wallpaper

to hold the cards and letters

from farther away than Christmas

with no return address

Equilateral Distance

origin of grief
vacuous isolation

my blood knows a
sea-change and
pulses from the root of
our fatal intersection

the steeper the slope
the faster I run
risking
grit in ripped skin
blood in the dust
of the trail
hands burned with
friction

fiction intercepts chaos
and waits
for the quiet rain
to calm the ashes
and settle the score

achieve equality

what you do to
one side you must
do to both

teeter totter
war games

explore the why
or end up with

Reading Your Name in My Inbox

under the canopy between my pelvic peaks
cumulus clouds turn themselves inside out
exhaling convex puffs that multiply and expand
to settle in the basin of my belly
waiting with little sighs
to be called to the surface by the moment
of your tongue (on my lips)
(your breath) on my neck
your voice (at the base of my skull)
rum-tumbling slowly down ladders of vertebrae
to melt in the marrow of my core

Lessons on Sleeping Alone

there has to be a trick

the virgin mattress still warm
from the Eastern European breath
of chiseled delivery men
crisp queen sheets tucked tightly
beneath the nickel plated headboard
posed like a crown on coronation day

I always used to leave the extra pillows
on one side
but now they seem too hopeful
and the wasted space too hollow and full
too ominous

and I begin to understand
the older women I know
who sleep in single twins
no pretense
no desire for company
carving a world on their own terms
with no room left for lovers

then my daughter falls asleep reading
in the middle of the bed
covers pushed asunder
and limbs splayed open and out
like nine years ago cradled and free
and I see she's kicked the extra pillows
onto the floor
so that her whole dancing self can
claim the space for dreams
and I note the critical difference
between waiting for something
off to one side
and the choice to make a little room
later on
if I feel like it

The Famous Writer in the Plastic Frame

he looks jaunty and slightly wicked
as he smolders
out of his low-resolution place of honor
next to the hand soap pump on the vanity

no doubt confusing the Christian woman
who cleans my house each month
and my daughter
who wonders who that man in the bathroom is

yet *I'm pretending he's my boyfriend*
seems to satisfy her and she resumes building
Lincoln Log civilizations across the kitchen floor

I am not a stalker
though I fixate on his picture and imagine
having sex with him on top of the washing machine
at the summer house on Nantucket

an unexpected tryst en route to the backyard BBQ
raw steaks forgotten on the shelf next to the Dreft

he takes me despite propriety
and the actual difference in our heights

on the back of book jackets he is much taller

Divorcing California Takes Time

growing up in Los Angeles
city of tamales and lucky cats waving from the top shelf
pasty white girl towering over brown friends
with killer serves on the court
white bread alphabetized between Fernandez and Gonzaga
power lines draping the streets like crepe paper and piñatas
hills green for twenty minutes in the spring and then wildfire ashes
falling on the playground at recess commingling with the smog
like cinnamon and sugar on a churro
we washed our hair every day rinsed and repeated

nighttime helicopters with searchlights like Hollywood
chuttering and chopping through the never-dark ET sky
glowing from movie stars' color TVs somewhere above
the big white sign behind their big white gates
where they washed the famous cement out from
under their fingernails

eyes straight ahead through the park
smell of funny smoke from the amphitheater
navigating between the cholos and the perverts
to get to Algebra before the second bell
safety in numbers
homecoming game in the Rose Bowl
makes me want to brag we were so cool
kicking Franklin's ass in our imaginations
spending New Year's Eve in the gutters making out and waiting
watching to confirm that our float was the bitchin'est of them all

city looks cleaner, tidier from the air above LAX
rusty Spanglish dusts itself off as the cabin pressure changes in my brain
while cravings for Ernie Jr's and Casa Bianca mix on my tongue
the spongy air washes over my high altitude dry skin
absorbing oleander and eucalyptus and sea salt and leaf-blower fumes

divorcing California takes time

Fish

her legs finally rejected
the underwater ground
defied habitual gravity and flotation
and kicked the length of the pool
navigating the deep and the shallow

her face remembered the water of the womb
and her gentle eyes opened to the magical
blue-marble underwater-world

pride dripped from her lashes
blue reflecting blue
rimmed with chlorine

seven summers of swimming lessons
and road-trip motel pools
puddled in an aquatic convergence
on the deck around her feet

Mama, it's just like flying!

in the name of harmony and conciliation

in the space between the marriages

in an effort to respect the stories other people
invent and then believe

the fictional fiction

the manufactured manifestation
of a million grains of rice

scattered like these words

left out for everyone to see and judge
or ignore and think not of

but the vanity and challenges of unbroken hearts

and the fields of boulders over which we scramble
away from each other

shift

(the little poem's been packed away to Poland
crammed in cattle cars and denied all food and drink)

we are done

Driving Past Autumn Aspen Groves

the uphill splash of tangerine
bursts out of the darker evergreen
to shimmer and pose
like the most audacious dancers
in a ballet of such grand scale
even truckers with their
tins of chew are rendered dumb
and forget the details of the road
as we are all brought closer to whole
closer to absolved
slightly more full of grace
than we were at summer's end

here's what's real

on this page

with the shit and the blood and the drool

that comes from the messy acts of human life

exactly from the beginning

with meconium and amniotic fluid and shreds of placenta

and the start of the beginning

with semen and mucus and sloughed-off uterine trash

seeping from our bodies as if it isn't obvious

that metaphor is fact

and symbols are simply accessories

we hang around our throats

and dangle from our ears

here's this poetry

here's what's real

outside the porcelain facades

of professionalism and accepted norms

our chemical selves in all our juicy mess

leave trails of truth shimmery as any snail's

a fierce, uncomplicated love

fueled first by the intensity
of shared blood and oxygen
and uterine real estate
and then by the added miracles
of profound regard and common joys

(this love is unrivaled —
free from issues of power or sex,
finances or careers)

and now

(as we sit in the ballpark
and eat our soft serve cones
and scream when the ball flies
over the centerfield wall,
stomping our feet with the contagious fervor
of the true fanatics that surround us)

my ribs swell and expand
against the context of my skin
stretched this time to contain
the softest, most ferocious tenderness

reflected in the golden moon of your face
your chin raised for a sticky kiss
your devotion crystallized
in your sturdy arms as you wrap me
in the ecstatic squeeze of camaraderie

knowing and being known
loving and being loved

setting*occasion*action

chest *(yours – concave)*
curled around spine *(mine – convex)*

arm draped over ribs
tucked under breast
terminating in fingers interlaced right and right

(safe)
I graze freely over the acreage of your heart
protected from predators *(though)*

the scars of battles fought and lessons won
still smart in the bright sunlight

(and so) you tuck your knees more tightly into mine
left arm up to touch my hair

face in my neck
voice in my ear
your kiss *(your whisper)*

frees me
(so nourished am I in the sanctuary of your embrace)

ten incisions
across the sternum
peeled back
like the sections
of an orange
cut into a star
pinned at the points
with rusty tacks
(the silver kind with flat heads)
into the flesh around my ribs
and my collarbones
and my breasts

movement in any direction
is impossible
without risking the symmetry
of the wound
tearing the flesh
indiscriminately

suspension, perhaps
in isolation
where the tacks could be replaced
with upholstery needles
and fishing line
pulled in equal
and opposite directions
beyond the confines
of the host body

unavailable for anything
but stillness and silence
and the paralysis
of the butterfly
pinioned to the foam core
of the entomologist's
shadow box

Deserted

circus bodies on the playa
contort through hoops of fire

this powerlessness
(it's not my scene)

you drive west toward kindred spirits
(leaving kin behind)

to call out Mephistopheles
daring the devil to show his face

looking for God
in heat waves on the horizon

in psychedelic spirit walks
blistering the earth

I pray behind the tulip beds
tended by the children last fall

while you carve your cathedral
out of sand
where no life exists
(no need to hang the food bag)

except in this one holy week
when pilgrims trek
carrying water and contraband
across state lines

(it's not my scene)

to tempt temptation
in the swirling heat
and the twirling bodies
and the dancing fire
and the thieving winds

(must remember to come home
and let the dog out)

walk carefully past the singing gypsies
with their dancing bells
and their sticky fingers

away from the open arms
of the painted women
for whom I do not exist
despite the indelible impression
of my body on your skin

(my wife's a poet
it's not her scene)

away from the edge
of life-as-you-know-it
(you cannot survive the fall
unscathed
unscarred
unforgiven)

the desert will drink us whole
leaving only shards of glass
and wooden splinters
where we were drops of oil

(it's not my scene)

Continental Breakfast

the fruit on my plate arranges itself
around the virtuous bran muffin
and the pious hard-cooked egg:
watermelon nestles
next to cantaloupe stained by strawberries
grapes are conspicuously absent
but the requisite honeydew
occupies its watery place
on the periphery of the plate

acolytes digest
the words of the keynote speaker
while chewing and spewing
into notebooks and laptops
and I

loner in the corner

horde the pineapple
like little yellow bricks of redemption
saving its pulpy rewards until
every other morsel is consumed
and the PowerPoint presentation comes
to its impotent climax
and the speaker sits down to sign his books
and then

only then
do I allow it to traverse my tongue
and lodge firmly
between my pencil and my teeth
receiving absolution in its transubstantiation
from simple fruit
to momentary miracle

the very much of alone
wears me like a coat
a vapor of fog surrounding
the surface area of myself

pushes past gravity
into the absence
of his height and breadth
the trunk of him in the center
of the forest of not here

now wraps in skeins of voids
pinning bows and arrows
between my arms at my sides
leaving only space for fingers
to caress quietly
keeping small company
in the interim

'Not in Vain Do We Watch the Setting
and Rising of the Stars'

I am Maria Mitchell
watching my daughter's comet tail
streak across the sky.

I stand firmly in the dark
on my nineteenth century planet
searching for
a telescopic glimpse
of her glimmering petticoats.

My darling comet
streaks on
into the riddles of the future.
I stand on rooftops
peering upward.

Telescopes, corsets, button hooks.
These are the tools
of my days.
Her unfathomable technologies
are yet to come.
Beyond comprehension.
Undecipherable tongues which
she'll speak fluently.

She will pause on earth to stand
at my headstone
and marvel at all
I could not have imagined.

'Oh, how she would have loved...'
she'll say,
gathering up her fiery skirts
and orbiting off into the celestial dark.

Racing to make the numinous known.

Suddenly Around the Bend

the Colorado river valley appears
like a banquet spread for our homecoming

Utah mesas recede in the rearview mirror
like distant temples
where we were exchange students

and we are coming home
although we've left home three states back
and felt at home in many hospitable berths

but this valley of green ranches and Bob Ross meadows
sloping from generous hills
and swirling in the shallows of the mudbrown water

this valley I notice

the map carves it up
yet when seen from the road
it simply beckons
and stretches like a friendly cat
come from the porch to greet the wanderer
and welcome her back

my boots will rest under a bed here tonight
and I'll ponder the question of home tomorrow

Why I Read Fiction

You've no interest
in things that never happened
to folks who don't exist

but every time
I turn the final page
(The End)

a timber bar
across a castle door
lifts up

the drawbridge
of a slightly broken heart
slides down

inviting you across
a brackish moat
into

my fortress of non-fiction
love

where I live and breathe and wait
only what's true

only for you

About the Author

Megan E. Freeman writes poetry and fiction. She has been published in poetry anthologies and literary and educational journals, including *Turtle Island Quarterly*, *Literary Mama*, *Green Fuse Poetic Arts*, and *English Journal*. Composer Steven Sametz selected her poem, *Music's Music*, as the text for a commission by the Los Angeles Master Chorale, which premiered at Disney Concert Hall. With degrees from Occidental College and The Ohio State University, Megan has over twenty years of experience teaching in the arts and humanities, and she is nationally recognized for her work leading professional development programs for educators. Megan has lived in northeast Los Angeles, central Ohio, northern Norway, and on Caribbean cruise ships. Now she lives near Boulder, Colorado.

Learn more at *www.meganefreeman.com*.

Appreciation

Many thanks to the following readers: Beckie Garrett, Mariamne and M.D. Friedman, Jen Dauzvardis, Shelby and Marcos Bradlina, Leah Rogers, Tiné De La Torre, Clara Quinlan, Dave Dugan, and Gary Grundei. Thanks to my long-time writing partners, Heather Preusser and Kristie Betts Letter, for their discerning eyes, sharp ears, wicked wits, and constant faith. Thanks to Chuck Ceraso for giving us *Tea for One* for the cover art, and to Ginny Downey for her generosity and love in creating the author photo. Thanks to Bob King, Jared Smith, and Veronica Patterson for spending time with the manuscript and crafting such lovely responses. And thanks to Liquid Light Press for a collaborative and joyful publishing experience. Thanks to my family, and especially to my parents, for teaching me to love language.

And thanks to Fiona Grace, for everything.

Other Books from Liquid Light Press

All Liquid Light Press books are available directly from *liquidlightpress.com* or from any of the current major global distribution channels including Amazon, Barnes and Noble, the iBookstore and the Ingram Catalog.

♥ *Leaning Toward Whole* by M. D. Friedman (2011) — Explores the poignant and personal. Also available as a groundbreaking multimedia enhanced e-book.

♥ *The Miracle Already Happening — Everyday Life with Rumi* by Rosemerry Wahtola Trommer (2011) — A superb collection of poems full of heart, humor, peace and wisdom.

♥ *Spiral* by Lynda La Rocca (2012) — A compelling poetic and melodic discourse of the persistent cravings and fears inside of each of us.

♥ *From the Ashes* by Wayne A. Gilbert (2012) — A true masterpiece that gnaws at the heart with universal appeal.

♥ *ah* by Rachel Kellum (2012) — This poetry has a simplicity and clarity that cuts to the core of being human.

♥ *Catalyst* by Jeremy Martin (2012) — *Catalyst* may just launch you on a fiery ride into yourself.

♥ *Of Eyes and Iris* by Erika Moss Gordon (2013) — Beautiful yet poignant in its simplicity.

♥ *Your House Is Floating* by Susan Whitmore (2013) — As smooth, crisp and satisfying as olive oil on fresh garden greens.

♥ *Nowhere Near Morning* by Jeffrey M. Bernstein (2013) — An intimate embrace of what it means to be alive.

♥ *Harmonica* by Cecele Allen Kraus (2014) — *Harmonica* bristles with a shimmering music that heals the heart.

♥ *Surf Sounds* by Roger Higgins (2014) — Expertly crafted and elegantly written, pulsing with the tides of the soul.

♥ *Black-Footed Country* by Lindsay Wilson (2015) — Like eating an artichoke, there are layers within thorny layers, each one more tender and subtle until you feast on the heart inside.

♥ *The Dice Throwers* by Douglas Cole (2015) — *The Dice Throwers* shines like a flashlight across the gritty dark alleys of the American soul, turning shattered glass into diamonds.